THE JOURNEY TO SUCCESS

ENGLISH EDITION OF DR. LUTFOR RAHMAN'S UNNOTO JIBON

MD. ABU BAKKAR

Contents

Preface

The Journey to Success is the English version of Dr. Lutfor Rahman's seminal Bengali prose work, *Unnoto Jibon.* This book is not just a collection of ideas; it is a blueprint for anyone seeking to rise above challenges and create a life of purpose, dignity, and achievement. In a world where success is often measured by external achievements and fleeting moments of recognition, I believe that true success is built on a foundation of inner strength, character, and perseverance.

As we journey through the chapters, you will explore the vital principles that drive success—not just in business, but in life itself. From the power of hard work, faith, and determination, to the importance of character, personal initiative, and keeping promises, this book offers practical wisdom that can be applied to every aspect of your existence.

The stories shared here are meant to inspire, the lessons are meant to teach, and the values are meant to serve as guiding lights on your path. In the face of adversity, it is not merely the resources at our disposal that determine our success, but rather the strength of our will, the resilience of our character, and the effort we put forth each day.

This book is a call to action, urging you to embrace the dignity of labor, the power of words, and the value of moral strength in all that you do. Each chapter aims to instill a sense of purpose and drive, encouraging you to cultivate not only your career but also your inner character.

Whether you are just beginning your journey or seeking to reaffirm the values that have guided you thus far, I hope you will find inspiration in these pages. The rise of a nation is not just about great leaders, but about the countless individuals who embody these same principles in their own lives, shaping the world in ways both big and small.

Let this book be a reminder that success is not just a destination—it is a journey of growth, effort, and unyielding determination.

Md. Abu Bakkar
(12 Feb 2025)

● vi ●

TRANSLATOR

Md. Abu Bakkar is a passionate educator and writer from Bangladesh. Born in 1991, he completed his elementary and secondary education in local institutions before pursuing higher studies in *English Language and Literature* at the International Islamic University Chittagong. He earned his BA (Hons) degree in 2013 and his MA degree in 2014, both in English Language and Literature.

In 2019, after years of dedication, Md. Abu Bakkar fulfilled his long-cherished dream of becoming a teacher. He began his teaching career as an English instructor at a high school in his home district. Since then, he has continued to inspire and guide students.

Recently, Bakkar has developed a deep interest in writing and translation. He is particularly drawn to translating classic works of literature that have stood the test of time and remain relevant across cultures and generations. Through his writing and translations, he aims to bridge the gap between languages and bring the beauty of literature to a wider audience.

Md. Abu Bakkar's passion for both teaching and translation reflects his commitment to fostering a love for literature and making timeless works accessible to all.

AUTHOR

Dr. Lutfor Rahman was born in 1889 in Jessore District, in British India. Lutfor Rahman was known for his efforts toward the improvement of women's society. He gained recognition as a thoughtful and rational essayist. His essays were clear, approachable, and serious in tone. He encouraged people to be attracted to the great thoughts of life through literature. His works reflect a deep sense of life, human values, high ideals, the truth of life, and an insightful analytical perspective.

In addition to his essays, Dr. Rahman wrote poems, novels, and children's literature. His literary journey began primarily with poetry. In 1915, he published his first and only poetry book, which included forty poems. Later, he wrote various essays, novels, short stories, articles, and children's literature. Some of his translation works have also been found.

Facing extreme poverty and suffering from a disease, the humanitarian writer Dr. Lutfor Rahman passed away on March 31, 1936, at the age of 47 without receiving any medical treatment.

I
The Rise of a Nation

If a nation is told—"Grow, wake up"—it seems that no good will come of such advice. A nation is essentially made up of individuals. Each person, known or unknown in the village, should be considered.

What is the way to make people strong, great, and developed? If we simply tell them, "Wake up," without anything else, they will not wake up. This advice is tied to many factors. It needs to be properly understood.

Again, I say—if we tell a nation from the outside, "Grow," it will not work. People must be considered individually.

A person, inspired by national sympathy, sent thousands of rupees to Turkey. When he would go out singing the tales of countless suffering people, every person's heart would fill with sympathy, sorrow, and compassion. But this person, after some time, had no hesitation in taking everything from a starving neighbor. It seems that such a stir of feeling and awareness of pain is of no great value. When a nation begins to fall, it is not that there are no public servants. I don't say no one sacrifices their life for the love of freedom; but those who care, their hearts slowly begin to blind. To make a nation truly great and self-sacrificing, how must every person in society become great and self-sacrificing? What is the way to instill a sense of self-awareness in the people of the country? How can every person become strong, developed, full of love, respectful of truth and justice, and disgusted by falsehood and lies? If a nation's people do not develop in this way, the nation will not grow.

We must create a natural yearning for knowledge within each person. The world functions in such a way that not everyone has access to school or higher education. Or, over the course of their schooling, many fail to obtain knowledge.

Some people grow up without fathers, some fathers do not consider education necessary and do not send their children to school, some become stubborn and rebellious during their studies and abandon learning, and some, thinking foreign languages are useless, stop studying altogether.

Out of five thousand students, only fifty remain, while the rest grow up ignorant, weak, and silent. This is a great loss for the nation.

The path to gaining humanity is the service of knowledge. In every situation of life—just like food and bathing—people need to serve knowledge.

An advanced, self-sacrificing, strong, loving, and just person cannot be found among the uneducated or undereducated. For a nation or a person to become great, they must constantly serve knowledge.

How can we make every person in the country knowledgeable? The backbone of a nation's life is humanity and knowledge. If we tell a nation to awaken while neglecting these two, it will not wake up.

Whether due to ignorance or the cycle of circumstances, if in any country, many people, due to illiteracy or limited education, become crude in mind and disrespectful of knowledge, then the life of that nation will not be sustainable. There is a way to awaken these dormant souls and a way to give them the power of speech. This method has always been effective everywhere, at all times. Without this method, no nation would have become strong or developed.

Nations have always followed this path to become strong. The Greek, Roman, and current European nations followed this path to attain greatness.

Those who neglect this path while trying to establish themselves are starting an impossible task.

This path is none other than the nurturing of the country's or nation's literature. A society that has no respect for literature is generally a barbaric society. Writing words down on paper for countless people to see is called the service of literature. These words are not just ordinary words—through them, the search for life is offered, the message of virtue and liberation is spread, and the doors to both present and ultimate happiness are opened.

These words take the form of songs and stories, sometimes poetry and philosophy, sometimes essays and science, appearing before people in colorful, sweet ways.

If someone walks along a dark, thorny, and perilous road without a lamp or mocks the necessity of light, what can be said about them? If any nation disregards literature or looks upon it with disdain, it will not develop.

To educate the educated further, to make the thoughtful even deeper, and to make the uneducated or semi-educated outside the centers of learning stronger, more knowledgeable, and filled with a sense of humanity, many great thinkers are born in every country.

They are the guides of the nation. They build the nation. The creators of civilization, the Greeks, Arabs, Hindus, and Europeans, are they.

Through the literature of every country, these educated classes lift the nation up. Hungry and distressed people become kings under their influence, the rural farmers, the unknown beggars in distant cottages, the servants of the landowners, the poor ox-cart drivers, the sinful in darkness, the cobblers of the market, the clockmakers in the city, the servants of the Nawabs, and the youth of the villages all become great figures through their teachings. To accept this wisdom, people must have some strength—some knowledge of letters. These people are the backbone of the nation—if they are denied, the nation loses its life force.

To make a nation strong, prosperous, wealthy, developed, and justly distribute wealth among the masses, books of all types, in both simple and complex languages, should be propagated in the country. The influence of the writings of powerful, visionary great figures can bring about a mental and earthly transformation in a nation in a relatively short period. Every person in the country learns to abandon their ignorance, superstitions, blindness, inertia, inferiority, and narrow-mindedness, and learns to adopt the idea of a higher life, full of humility and wisdom. They establish humanity and justice as their religion, gain self-respect, and become deeply nourished. Then, great power awakens.

Behind the great strength of the British lies the power of many writers. In fact, writers and scholars quietly, behind the scenes, give direction to all global events and endeavors. Their unseen hand causes countless people to create oceans in the desert and raise mountains in the sea—the creators of world civilization are they.

If the people of any country fail to respect this class of
writers or national literature, they are truly low. If the scholars of the nation are killed, the entire nation will become powerless.

If you wish to turn a civilized nation into an uncivilized one, then destroy their books, kill all the scholars, and your purpose will be fulfilled.

Writers, poets, and scholars are the soul of a nation. Those who neglect this soul do not live.

If you wish to develop a country or nation, it must be done through the help of literature. Of all the activities for human well-being, this is the most important and complete. Create a current of literature within the nation, and nothing else is necessary. If you desire to make a nation civilized and human, then work to improve the literature of that country in accordance with its rules and systems. Literature in the mother tongue must be developed. Foreign literature does not bring any benefit to the general welfare of humanity. National literature must be developed, and at the same time, the essence of the world's great literature must be collected. If you are satisfied with what you have and do not seek to improve it, the path to the nation's progress becomes blocked.

All of humanity's problems are solved through literature.

When a nation becomes perceptive and knowledgeable, it does not wait for someone to call it to wake up, because awakening becomes its nature.

*****

II

The Success of Personality and Strength

Wherever you are, try to grow and develop on your own. Believe that in every situation in life, you can elevate yourself.

Before thinking of nationalism and independence, make yourself a true human being. Without the development and refined growth of an individual's personality, independence is nothing. One person said, "When I think of the word freedom, I cannot help but think of the self-improvement of each individual in the country."

Strengthen your own personality. No one can dominate you unjustly — this is what the philosopher Mill said.

If you harm yourself, if you start torturing yourself with ignorance and sin, who will make you great? You work for yourself, and your friends are not low. Practice the strength inside you, and you will become a great person.

Just because you were born into a poor family, do not let anyone reduce you. They are the small ones. You are human, with a soul inside you, and that is enough. Believe that you are not small.

Even the greatest kings may not leave behind a legacy. Education is not just for a class of well-mannered people. In fact, there is no such thing as "well-dressed" people. Even those who are small, insignificant, and humble, can be refined and they also have power, and they should believe that.

Through education, knowledge, character, and hard work, you can become worthy of respect, even if you are poor. No matter what your situation is, acquire knowledge and work hard. People will respect you. You may be a merchant, a small tailor, or in a corner of the world — if you are virtuous and have character, you will gradually improve in all aspects — your respect and wealth will grow.

Meher Ullah was a humble tailor from Jessore.

Do not be disappointed if you failed an exam, or if you couldn't enter school or college. People want character, knowledge, personality, and strength.

In human society, on roads, in shops, in trains, and on steamers — if you observe carefully, you can acquire immense knowledge. Awaken your ability to think, and your vision will open. With that vision, you will see everything inside and out, and you will become a true person.

The college just shows you the way — you must look, learn, and acquire knowledge throughout your life.

The college does not aim to make you selfish, cunning, greedy for money, or a thief. It's not for building houses, becoming a police officer, or digging ponds to gain social prestige. The college shows you the path of duty in life; it teaches you to be perceptive, responsible, virtuous, self-reliant, humble, and courageous. If you focus on this goal, you will shape yourself and won't need to go to college.

It's great if you get the chance to go to college or school. But if that's not possible, don't despair. You don't have to stay small. You can grow through effort at any point in life and at any age. You are human, you are a spark of fire, you cannot fall, and you cannot be destroyed. Do not dishonor your life in exchange for money or worldly pleasures.

Shakespeare was the son of a humble man. If he had been born in our country, people would have called him the son of a low-class person. Yet, the great man to whom the English nation owes much of its strength and civilization was born a humble man. Through the pursuit of knowledge, he was able to give his personality a great place, which is difficult to compare with anyone.

Do you know the name of Dr. Livingstone? Livingstone was a poor person.

Naval expert Sir Cloudesley Shovell, scientist Sturgeon, writer Samuel Dray, and priest William Carey were all ordinary people.

Through their hard work, they have left a mark in the world, a mark that even the greatest men could not leave. Indeed, without work and accomplishment, the greatest men have no value.

In a coastal town, an English boy worked in a tailor's shop. A warship was passing by, and the boy, like any other child, went to see it. He was so inspired by the ship's sight that he immediately decided to join it. He rushed to the ship's captain and, after seeing his enthusiasm, the captain accepted him. This humble tailor's boy eventually became an Admiral.

At one time, the leader of the United States, Andrew Johnson, was mocked for being a former tailor. He responded without shame, saying, "I was a tailor, but I always did the right thing and never wronged anyone."

No matter what work you do, there is no shame in it. Shame comes from earning money in dishonest ways, begging, or being foolish. Gain knowledge, awaken the power within you, and you will not remain small.

Make yourself great, and the world will recognize your greatness. Make yourself worthy of respect in your own eyes, and people will respect you. Who do people bow down to? Who do they show reverence to?

George Stephenson was a coal miner.

Newton was the son of a farmer. Milton's father was a peasant.

Sir Humphry Davy said that his position was the result of his efforts. When King Adrian was a child, he could not afford to buy oil for reading. He would read under the street lights. This patience and effort made him great — not destiny.

Mr. Fox, when he began speaking, would always start by saying, "When I was a boy working in a weaving mill in Norwich..."

Many great people of England came from humble beginnings. Through hard work and the pursuit of knowledge, they were able to become great people. Why can't you?

*****

III

Perseverance, Hard Work, Faith, and Patience

Whatever work you do, you will not necessarily succeed at it the first time. You must overcome failure through effort. Keep trying, keep striking again and again, your efforts will bear fruit.

Who has ever become great by luck? Without perseverance and hard work, who has gained wealth and honor?

Even great people have achieved glory and respect through many years of patience and effort. Those who do not fear failure and work with the belief that they will succeed are the ones who ultimately succeed. If you do not know how to read, but you have just these two qualities—perseverance and faith—then you can become great!

Many people do extraordinary things through talent, but in comparison to years of patient effort, talent holds no value. Work calmly, stay steady, and fulfill your duties. Talent will feel embarrassed in the face of your perseverance.

Many people have been born in this world. Among them, hardworking people far outnumber the talented ones. One writer has said that talent is simply patience and hard work.

Newton said, "The reason for my discoveries is not my talent. Through years of hard work and continuous concentration, I have succeeded. When something came to my mind, I was engrossed in solving it. I have gradually moved from uncertainty to clarity."

Dr. Bentle told him once, "If any benefit has come to humanity through me, it is through many years of patient effort."

Voltaire said, "There is no such thing as talent. Work hard, persevere, and you will be able to recognize talent."

People say that not everyone can become a poet. Becoming an orator is also a gift from God, but I don't believe that.

People called Dalton talented, but he denied it and said, "Without hard work, I know nothing."

Nothing is impossible in the face of hard work, observation, and patient effort.

Those who have built the world and society were not necessarily exceptional or gifted. They were hardworking and patient practitioners.

If talent is not illuminated by perseverance or effort, it will not be honored. It will not make a significant impact on the world.

When Sir Robert Peel was a child, his father would place him on a small table and ask him to give speeches. Initially, he didn't succeed, but through repeated efforts, the boy's ability emerged. In his later years, he said that his extraordinary eloquence and debating skills were honed during his childhood efforts.

Stay calm and persistent, you will not have to suffer. Persistence is the path to success. Never give up, your boat will rise.

To do good work, you cannot be impatient. Whatever the task is, a musician was once asked by a youth how long it would take to learn music. He replied, "If you work hard for 12 hours every day, it will take twenty years."

One scholar said, "The person who waits patiently is the one who will succeed." How long one must wait, no one knows. With hope in your heart and faith in God, keep working, you will succeed.

Fill your perseverance with joy. Do not worry about when you will succeed. If you do, you will grow weary in your efforts. Failure will break you, but with joy and indifference to the immediate results of your efforts, your mind will gradually take you to your goal. In the bright morning, you will find your head adorned with the crown of victory. You will be astonished by your own success.

Do not do any work with despair and lack of joy. Like the tireless Reverend William Carey, he was also full of hope and faith in his work. The Serampore College was established through his effort.

Once, this great man was ridiculed by someone who called him the cobbler's son. Carey replied, "I am not at all ashamed of that."

In his youth, he once fell from a tree and broke his leg. After a few months, he got up from bed and climbed the same tree again, without hesitation. This is the special feature of the lives of great men!

Philosopher Young said, "What man has done, man can do." There is an interesting story related to this. One day, he was riding a horse with a friend. It was his first time riding, and his friend, an experienced rider, jumped over a high fence with ease. Young wanted to do the same, but for someone who had never ridden before, it wasn't easy. He tried to jump but fell off the horse. Without losing heart, he tried again. This time he didn't fall, but had to hold on tightly to the horse's neck. He tried again, and this time he succeeded.

After working for twenty years, Newton wrote a book. His favorite dog knocked over a lamp, and the book was burned to ashes in an instant. Twenty years of effort and thought were destroyed in an instant. Newton was deeply saddened, but what remarkable patience he showed! He did not give up and started writing the book again and finished it.

Carlyle wrote the history of the French Revolution and let a neighboring writer read it. The writer accidentally left it outside, and it was lost. Upon investigation, it was found that the housemaid had burned the precious book, thinking it was waste paper.

When Carlyle heard this terrible news, one can only imagine his mental state.

It is impossible to describe the pain Carlyle endured while rewriting the book. There was no alternative but to rewrite it. With great perseverance and mental strength, he wrote the book again. Carlyle's patience and mental strength are nothing short of astonishing. George Stephenson used to tell his sons, "What should I tell you? Follow me—strike again and again!"

Watts worked for thirty years and left the world indebted to him. Thirty years of effort is not a small thing! His work, done with persistence, showed how much greatness can come from steady, hard work. He said, "Talent means patience and hard work." Buffon, despite his lack of memory, lived a very good life. His habits had made him lazy, and he would sometimes lie in bed for a long time. After much contemplation, he could not escape from this bad habit. Finally, he told his servant Joseph, "From tomorrow, wake me up early. Give me one dollar as a reward for each day you wake me up." The next day, Joseph tried to wake him up, but got slapped and hit in return. Buffon scolded Joseph for not doing his job properly. Joseph was determined that the next day he would make sure Buffon got up. The next morning, he went to Buffon's bed, and Buffon angrily said, "I am sick. I didn't sleep well last night—go, don't disturb me." If the servant disobeys, he will lose his job, and Joseph left.

The next day, Joseph, undeterred, went to wake Buffon up again. Buffon, refusing to rise, Joseph poured a bucket of cold water on Buffon's bed, forcing him to get up. Joseph earned his reward!

Buffon worked diligently for nine hours a day for forty years. He couldn't live without working. It had become his habit. His biographer wrote that work was his favorite thing more than play. He never had trouble reading incessantly.

He revised and wrote the same book several times. No other writer has perhaps ever been able to revise their work as much as Buffon.

He spent fifty years thinking and wrote a book. Remarkably, he was still not satisfied. Once, twice—he rewrote the book eleven times.

No one had more patience than Buffon. Even in the midst of suffering, he wrote great books. Being at work was his joy and peace.

Sir Walter Scott was hardworking. Alongside his office work, he contributed to knowledge and literature. His office duties were no small task, and on top of that, his literary contributions demanded great effort!

At five in the morning, he would wake up and start the stove himself. After eating a little, he would sit down with his books, ready to serve literature. Before his children, wife, and in-laws woke up, he had already completed a lot of work.

Despite many years of hard work and deep learning, Scott would say, "I cannot help but feel ashamed when I think of my ignorance."

A student went to a professor at Trinity College and earned his B.A. degree. He said, "Sir, my studies are over. How much longer should I work? I'll go home and rest now." The professor, surprised, replied, "Your knowledge has ended? I have only just begun."

Those who know little often feel their work is finished. The great scholar Newton, at the end of his life, said, "Standing at the shore of the ocean of knowledge, I have only stirred up a little dust. I have seen nothing of the vast ocean."

John Britton's uncle threw him out of the shop, leaving him utterly helpless. When Britton was young, his father went mad. His father was a bread-seller.

Britton lived with his hotel-owner uncle and worked there. He earned some money, but suddenly he fell ill, and his health deteriorated to the point where he couldn't work anymore. His cruel uncle couldn't bear this loss. He threw a few coins into Britton's hands and said, "You don't need to stay here anymore."

The seven-year-old Britton's hardships were unimaginable. Yet, he never gave up studying. Even though he couldn't go to school, he never sat idly. He kept learning in every way he could.

Those who have knowledge and power, whether they succeed in passing something or not, will surely attain a higher place in society. This is well known in Britain.

Reading Britton's biography reveals the immense struggles of his life. The house he lived in was very humble. There were times when he had no shoes. In the harsh cold, he sometimes went without covering. He had no money in his pockets. Even without money, he could not afford to neglect his studies. For a few minutes, he would study from borrowed books to satisfy his thirst for knowledge.

At the age of twenty-eight, he made his debut as an author. For the next fifty years, he served literature. John Britton wrote a total of seven hundred books. No obstacle could make his life a failure.

You are the master of your life—don't consider sorrow, pain, and poverty as obstacles. Rather, accept them as blessings. Nothing will stop your progress. Whatever happens, you will surely succeed. Even if your heart is broken—don't worry. With a broken heart, stand firm with trust in God.

Near Edinburgh, there was a boy named Loudon. His father was a farmer. The father wanted his son to learn gardening. Loudon had to do hard physical labor during the day. Despite this, he spent two nights a week staying awake to study.

Loudon had a strong desire to improve his life and make it glorious by doing good for mankind.

In a short time, this young boy with high aspirations mastered the French language. Once he knew French, he became eager to learn German. He quickly mastered the German language as well.

There were two other boys named Samuel and Zebez. Their father was a laborer. The poor father sent his two sons to the same school. Zebez had a great memory, but Samuel was mischievous and foolish. Seeing no progress in his studies, his father sent him to a shoemaker to learn the trade. There, under the pressure of work, his mind started to blossom.

Samuel had a keen interest in mischief and stealing. Once, in an act of mischief, he drowned in the sea, losing his life. But astonishingly, he managed to swim two miles to shore and saved himself.

After this incident, Samuel's nature changed completely. Who would have thought that this mischievous, thieving, hot-headed youth would one day amaze the world with his knowledge and wisdom?

After this life-changing incident, his wild and impulsive nature turned toward improvement. From then on, Samuel dedicated himself to study. The more he read, the more ashamed he became of his ignorance and foolishness. A powerful desire to eliminate this ignorance awakened inside him! The time he used to spend earning a living was now devoted to studying. He never allowed even a minute to be wasted. When he couldn't find time to study because of work, he would sit down during meals and read a book.

After reading a certain book, his mind became more refined, and he became spiritually enlightened.

After some time, he started his own business. Afraid of debt, he sometimes went to bed hungry.

During the time he saved from business, literature, and study, he would give speeches in front of the public.

When he got married and had children, amidst the noise of his family, he would sit down to write and read.

In his later years, he said, "I have pulled myself up from a wretched state. My companions in this effort were hard work, character, and frugality."

*****

IV
Business, Industry, and Commerce

I once saw in a watchmaker's shop that his son had made an excellent machine. I never knew that such things were possible in our country.

A person from West Banani, Dhaka, showed me some handmade shell jewelry inside a steamer. I was amazed by these creations.

In many places, even an uneducated cobbler makes excellent shoes. Many people in the Indian subcontinent create beautiful and remarkable things. However, they do not receive appreciation because they cannot compete in the face of the power of science.

People in Britain have always had a strong inclination towards creating various household comforts and luxuries. They never sit idle with a single thought or result in mind. They continuously strive for further improvement. Our people do not do that. They do not think about what is necessary. In Bardhaman district, the work of making fine goods or the flower picking in Shantipur are not respected by the people of the country.

In business, there is much more benefit to the survival of a nation. Education or knowledge is not for securing a job. Using knowledge to improve in every area, you can become a good farmer, blacksmith, tailor, mechanic, and craftsman. Believe me, knowledge is not for getting a job. Just as you have hands and feet, knowledge should also be a part of you. Do not acquire knowledge just for a job.

Being a craftsman or a businessman doesn't mean you must remain small. You must be diligent and hardworking in every field. I will tell you about a few people whose life stories will show you how they, through persistence, intelligence, and hard work, advanced in industry and trade, and helped improve their own lives, their country, and humanity. When obstacles appeared on their path, they did not let them stop them. The severe punishment of disrespect for industry and commerce is something people must endure forever!

Even if you are illiterate, if you are diligent, thoughtful, and perceptive, you can be of service to others. Through your innovative power, talent, and discoveries, you can benefit the people of the world forever.

Do business with a sense of virtue—earn your livelihood through hard work. Your position will never be low. Reject a life filled with fraud and lies, and embrace honest work. Learn to despise a useless life and to honor a true one. This is where your humanity lies. Many memorable individuals from merchant families have contributed greatly to the world. The main reason for national prosperity is the merchant's hard work and intelligence. The son of a mechanic, Watt's invention has done much to improve the world. The civilization of the world owes much to him. Who knew that the bump that rises from boiling water would have so much power? What cannot be achieved with the strength of a thousand horses can be accomplished through the bump's energy. If Watt had not shared this knowledge, the world's civilization would not have progressed as it has. The speed of trains, printing presses, and even wars are all driven by steam power.

As a result of Watt's discovery, Arkwright was able to develop an advanced spinning machine. Arkwright was not from a wealthy family. He was born in Preston in 1732. His father's condition was very poor. Arkwright was the youngest of thirteen children. He never had the chance to attend school, but he learned a little on his own.

At first, his father sent him to work in a barber's workshop. After learning the trade, Arkwright opened his own shop and also started a wig-making business. He would travel from town to town, buying and selling wigs. This business didn't succeed. Facing failure, Arkwright thought that the solution was to invent a better and more efficient machine to make thread. He then worked day and night, thinking about it. His earnings stopped, and his situation became miserable. He had already gotten married, but his wife could not tolerate his obsession and one day, she threw all his tools out of the house. Arkwright became furious, and this led to a permanent separation between them. He had no shirt to wear, no shoes, and his clothes were torn—but he didn't care. He kept thinking about how to invent a machine that could make thread using steam power.

Nothing can stop someone with unwavering dedication. Arkwright's efforts were not in vain. He established the main foundation of world civilization.

Arkwright's strength of character was limitless. His ability to work hard was extraordinary. After this discovery, he established large factories. He had to work tirelessly in these factories from early morning until nine at night.

When he was fifty years old, he started studying English grammar because, until then, he did not have the ability to write even two lines properly.

He gained wealth and glory. He benefited humanity. To honor his great life, the emperor awarded him a title.

One of Britain's greatest men, Sir Robert Peel, was once the minister to Emperor George IV. His father was a poor farmer. As it became difficult to provide for his large family, Peel's father began weaving cloth. At that time, there were no factories for making cloth in Britain. People used to weave at home. Peel's father was a humble and hardworking man. While doing this business, he became interested in inventing a method for printing patterns on cloth. After much thought, effort, and failure, like Arkwright, he succeeded. With human effort, perseverance, and thought, nothing is impossible.

Sir Robert Peel said about his father, "He was an intelligent and perceptive man. It was through him that the prosperity of our family began. The nation's progress depends on business. The prosperity of all the people in the country depends on business. A few people's small improvements don't matter here."

At the age of twenty, Peel started a business with a few broken houses and only a few hundred pounds.

The humble, hardworking, and frugal Peel gradually grew and opened new factories in many places.

Wealth, honor, and millions of pounds later, Peel had once been a laborer. Through virtue, hard work, and perseverance, he became a respected man in his country.

*****

V

Effort and Hard Work

There is no progress in the world without effort and hard work. Never believe that you will get a large sum of money through sheer luck. No matter what work you do, to gain true proficiency, you must practice for many years.

Do not despise the small or insignificant. It is through the small that the great is created. If you make use of small moments, you will reap gold in life. No one becomes great overnight. No one suddenly achieves success. Even if they do, do not believe it and make yourself weak.

Cowards look to fate, but men look to their own strength. It is not your luck that will elevate you, but your own determination—your strength and willpower, not fate.

Time passes day by day—those who are great in the world cannot tolerate waste.

When Watt was sitting in his shop selling goods, he spent that time studying chemistry and the German language, and became an expert in both fields. You might be surprised to hear this. Stephenson, while feeding coal into the engine, was also solving math problems.

Every time you waste on laughter and jokes, just remove one hour from it. If you spend that one hour wisely, in discussion or learning, after ten years you will have become a great scholar. Your respect among friends and companions will have grown. Perhaps you will have learned the entire history of the world, gained immense knowledge in mathematics, become a famous homeopathic doctor, or memorized the entire Quran or Bhagavad Gita.

Dr. Mason, while traveling in a carriage, translated a large book. Dr. Darwin wrote most of his books while traveling. Dr. Burne, while teaching a student Italian grammar, found time to write music.

A clerk of a lawyer learned the Greek language while going to the office from his home. When called to dinner, Dejes would always be late. This means that during that time, he was writing a book. He never wasted any time, even the time before meals.

The blacksmith Elihu Buritt, sitting in a well-maintained shop, became a scholar in thirty modern and ancient languages.

If you were to receive 500 rupees on the road, your joy would know no bounds. But time, a priceless gem, is tied around your feet, and yet you give it no thought. If you ask for money from people, they will despise you. But time, with its riches, stands at your door—accept its gifts with gratitude.

Some young men once went to meet Baxter and said, "Sir! We are afraid we are wasting your time." The wise Baxter replied, "Certainly."

The wise are always gathering jewels and pearls from the fields of time. You and I are standing idly, waiting for an opportunity, or using false excuses like lack of time or poverty. Work—work—always work in all conditions and at all times, and you will see the results. At first, your hard work might not bear fruit—but do not be discouraged. Before the famous writer Edison gained glory by writing the *Spectator*, he had written bags of useless papers. Though those papers remained in a useless room, it was within those writings that the foundation for his glory and progress was established.

*****

VI

The Seat of Dignity and Excellence - Pursuit of One's Strength

No family can remain forever intact with old dignity and respect. Just as a nation falls, so does a family.

Education, character, and knowledge honor both individuals and families, raising them in respect and stature in every way. When a person becomes ignorant and characterless, they lose their dominance and respect.

You may be small today—be virtuous and knowledgeable, and you too will become great. There is nothing written on your forehead that makes you polite.

Do you know how great the Muslim nation once was? The world used to take pride in following their civilization. What caused their downfall?

Until recently, people considered Japan uncivilized. But through effort, they now occupy a high place in the world. What is the value of our nose being deformed?

Today, you may consider a family insignificant—the results of their effort and hard work you may look at with disdain. In a short while, you may have to beg for their mercy. Your son may have to work as a servant in their house! In this world, only effort, character, and knowledge triumph. Fools, beggars, and pretentious gentlemen have no value. Don't seek recognition through your father's name! Do not boast that you were born in a good family.

The landlords who once treated Emperor John as their puppet—none of them remain alive.

A descendant of Emperor Edward I was once seen selling meat. A descendant of the Duke of Clarence was working as a cobbler in the city. A member of the great landlord Simon's family in Britain was making horseshoes in London.

Those who once held the greatest positions in the past now see their strength and respect reflected in new individuals.

Are you small? Through greatness, effort, and life's struggles, you will become victorious—let the development of knowledge and humanity reside in you—and you will attain a great position.

Richard, a poor young farmer, worked in a factory in Britain. The factory produced iron nails, but the business began to decline. This was because cheaper, stronger nails were coming from Sweden. Richard, working at the factory, thought about how he could make nails as cheap and strong as those from Sweden.

Some time passed, and suddenly Richard was not seen at the factory. Everyone thought he had stayed home due to laziness. In reality, he had secretly disguised himself and embarked on a ship to Sweden with a great purpose in mind: to save this profitable business and preserve his country's wealth. He had the ability to sing! When he reached Sweden, he enchanted the workers with his singing and managed to gain permission to stay in the factory. People began to think he was foolish, only capable of singing. No one suspected him.

Without raising suspicion, Richard observed how they made nails and what set their factory apart. Years passed in this manner. One morning, the factory workers noticed that their longtime companion, the "fool," was no longer there.

Once Richard had learned all the techniques for nail-making, he left.

Upon returning to his homeland, everyone learned of his reason for disappearing to Sweden, and the businessmen, encouraged by the prospect of profits, made Richard the manager of a large factory. Machines were set up according to his instructions, but unfortunately, the factory did not run smoothly. Everyone became disheartened, and Richard, too, was unprepared for the failure. He wondered if all the effort, money, and hard work had been in vain. But Richard's faith and determination did not falter.

He realized that his observations had been flawed. He once again secretly left for Sweden.

After many years, when he returned, the factory workers were happy to see their old friend. This time, with greater attention and focus, Richard resumed observing their factory. Many more years passed.

Through perseverance, attention, and effort, all the mistakes were resolved, and Richard, now well-prepared, left once again.

This time, he did not have to be unprepared.

He laid the path for a highly profitable business in England. As a result of his immense efforts, the nation's wealth grew considerably.

Emperor Charles II, recognizing this self-sacrificing man's qualities, conferred upon him the title of Sir. The son of a humble farmer had now attained the seat of England's greatest scholars.

The life story of William Phillips is truly remarkable. A mere shepherd boy, William was honored by the emperor through his own strength. It is no small feat for a shepherd to attain the country's highest title. People do not neglect strength and virtue, as it harms them. Strength and virtue are the great man's support—whether one knows their father's name or not, in the eyes of God, only virtue holds value.

William's father worked as a gunsmith. William and his 25 brothers worked together to help their father. William tended cattle. His life was that of a shepherd, but his inner strength was dormant.

His desire was to play with the stormy sea waves. His childhood heart longed to travel across the endless blue seas. When no opportunities arose, he began learning the craft of shipbuilding from a shipwright. In a short time, he became skilled in shipbuilding. During his spare time, he read books. Once he mastered the craft, he started building ships in Boston. Here, he married a widow.

The business was doing well. One day, while walking on the road, he overheard a conversation about a ship that had been filled with goods but had sunk in the sea. Whoever could recover the ship would be rewarded with millions of dollars.

Just as fire ignites when it touches ghee, this news sparked a flame of hope and enthusiasm in William's heart. If the sunken ship could be recovered, it would bring immense wealth.

William immediately gathered sailors and resources, and went to the site of the shipwreck, which was near the Bahamas.

William's hope and hard work did not go in vain. He found the sunken ship and recovered many valuable items. However, after the considerable expenses, there was not much profit.

After some time, William heard rumors of another shipwreck. This ship, sunk almost fifty years ago, was believed to have been carrying a vast quantity of jewels. Based on these rumors, William decided to venture into the sea again, seeking more treasure.

William's situation was not great. Even though he had some wealth, taking on such an expensive endeavor seemed impossible for one person.

Seeing no other option, he went to Emperor Charles II for help, presenting his case. The emperor, impressed by his enthusiasm and faith, agreed to assist him.

With renewed determination, William set sail once again in search of treasure. Those who accompanied him were equally enthusiastic, confident they would return home with great wealth.

Arriving at the designated location, William and his crew began searching the depths of the sea. Searching for treasure in the unknown depths of the ocean is no simple task.

Months passed in exhaustion and effort, but no significant results came. Slowly, the sailors began to grow restless. However, William's belief did not waver.

With the help of a loyal employee, William discovered that a conspiracy was being hatched to throw him into the sea. The ship had also suffered damage at various places. In the end, due to several reasons, William had to return.

Upon his return to England, William shared new information he had gathered about the sunken ship. His enthusiasm hadn't waned at all—he was eager to set out again, this time with new people. But this time, his words and beliefs held no value with the Emperor.

Therefore, William tried to raise funds for the second voyage from the public. But who would trust him? It took him four long years to win back the trust of the common people. After four years of effort, some of them decided to believe in him.

With the public's financial help, William set out again after four years, arriving back at the site with a new ship. Just like before, days and months passed, searching the sea floor. William sometimes began to wonder whether his belief had been in vain.

Then, one day, a diver came up from the water and said he had felt something like the deck of a ship. Filled with great anxiety, William sent a few more divers. Within moments, one came to the surface with a piece of gold. William clapped his hands in joy and thanked God, saying, "Our fortune has turned—no more fear!"

All the hard work, hope, and faith hadn't been in vain.

In just a few days, they recovered 4.5 million pounds from the sunken ship.

When William returned to England, many told the Emperor that William had no claim to the money, as it belonged to the royal treasury. They suggested that because William had not informed the government properly, all his money should be confiscated.

But the just Emperor, not paying heed to these words, honored his hard work and perseverance. He awarded William the title of "Sir" and bestowed upon him the highest honor.

William remained humble and simple until his last days. He never hid his past life from anyone. He had been born into a poor family, but through his own strength, he had earned the highest position and respect in England—he always felt proud to say this.

I know of a great soul named William Petit. His father had a clothing store. Petit was a university student in France. The way he financed his college and personal expenses will inspire many of you. Have you ever seen small, charming shops on the streets of Kolkata? Petit, in a similar manner, used to sell goods on the streets to fund his student life.

After completing his studies, he returned to his country and took a job on a ship. But this job didn't suit him.

One day, the captain of the ship insulted him, even striking him. Overcome with disgust and shame, Petit quit the job and went to Pauri city to study medicine.

In Pauri, he faced severe hardships. He had to sometimes lie with his stomach empty, filled only with water.

Despite this suffering and poverty, he managed to save a few coins. Petit began to sell goods on the streets again. With this income, he completed his medical studies.

Along with medicine, he began to serve literature. Gradually, his strength and talent gained recognition everywhere, and he earned the respect of the people. He began to make a living. He wrote articles on various subjects—sometimes on the complex theories of philosophy, sometimes on mathematics, sometimes on methods of cloth-making, or on techniques for preparing paints.

Petit had earned a considerable amount of money through business. The Emperor acknowledged his virtues and abilities with respect. The Emperor had awarded William Petit with the highest honor.

Nelson and Wellington were not from noble families—but they became the fathers of the British nation. One British lord once pointed to a small, damp hole of a house and said to his son, "Your grandfather used to work as a cobbler in that house. He was a barber—now I have become a Lord. It is through strength and hard work that one grows. I brought you here to show you this."

One of the greatest men of the 19th century, Gokhel, was born to a poor family. Through his own strength, he gained high positions and respect not only in India but abroad as well. He did not accept the title of "Sir" but was recognized for his contribution. The poor Gokhel achieved a high position through his own efforts.

Emperor Subuktasin was a slave. So were Qutbuddin and several other emperors. They had come from the life of slavery to become emperors—great servants of humanity, protectors of the world's religion, civilization, and peace.

*****

VII
The Power of Will and Determination

Whatever work you undertake, if you can put your heart and mind into it, there is no fear. Do not allow doubt to take root in your mind. Doubt weakens the mind, and success in any task becomes impossible.

When you decide to do something, believe in it—you will succeed. After that, work hard, and success will be yours.

I know of a person in France who walked around his house saying, "I will become a great warrior," and indeed, he became one.

There is a student I know, from a few years ago. He was feverish when he sat down to study. There was an upcoming exam—he knew he couldn't afford not to study. If he failed, it might even mean his life was at risk. Despite his fever, he forgot about it and started studying. Soon, his fever disappeared.

There was a gentleman who became ill. He decided that he must recover immediately, and indeed, he did recover.

Everyone knows the story of Emperor Babur. He managed to absorb his son's illness into himself.

Once, a military commander fell severely ill. Suddenly, a war broke out. Forgetting about his illness, he summoned an inhuman strength and fought in the battlefield. After victory, he passed away.

Will simply wishing make it happen? No, it is essential to wish firmly and believe—you will succeed. Dedication will come naturally. Do not fear sorrow, do not be defeated by poverty—through endless, unwavering determination, you will clear your own path.

With belief and strong will, the impossible becomes possible. If you are determined to succeed, pour your whole mind into the task—believe with all your heart that you will succeed. Remove doubt and disbelief from your heart. Those who are doubtful are cowards, and their efforts hold no value—they will be defeated.

One sage said, "We can become whatever we wish to be." This desire to become something must be strong and resolute.

One day, a craftsman made a chair and said, "I made this chair to sit on." He promised, "I will sit in this chair." To everyone's amazement, the craftsman, in time, became a respected person and sat in the very chair he had made.

You must not think of yourself as weak or powerless. You are human—inside you is the power that even mountains bow to, and the whole world trembles before it.

Are you in trouble? What is there to fear? Laugh at your troubles—cast aside the sting of poverty, and stand tall. You can reach the heights of success.

I know a man. A cruel gentleman once told him, "Take this stone on your head and carry it to the side of the road. Then, I will know that you are a strong man, and you will receive ten rupees as a reward." The man, driven not by money but by the desire for honor, set off carrying the stone on his head with great enthusiasm. But after going halfway, his face turned pale, his chest pounded in pain, and his eyes turned bloodshot.

A gentleman, out of curiosity and sympathy, followed him. Upon seeing the man's state, he approached him and said, "What is it? You can't go any further? Do you want to drop the stone? What are you saying?"

The gentleman, in a firm voice, said, "What? A man like you, strong as a rock, can carry this stone easily. Why drop it? Come, let's continue. I will go with you."

Encouraged by the gentleman's words, the man carried the stone to its destination with renewed energy and belief.

From the beginning of your life, decide what you are suited for. If you keep changing your direction, your life will never progress. Many people have ruined their lives this way—don't let that happen to you.

If you choose to be a businessman, pour all your energy into business. If you have doubts, then don't enter business—you will become frustrated within a few days. Your energy will be wasted. If your heart is not in it, you won't succeed in your work. If there's a will, there's a way—this proverb exists in the minds of all people.

If you have a strong desire to do something, no obstacle can stop you. You need only your will and belief. With this belief, you will receive the strength of God.

In religion, anyone who desires something deeply will get it.

Napoleon once said, "There is nothing impossible in this world." When Dr. Livingston was young, he went to work in a factory. The first week's wages were used to buy a Latin grammar book. Today, we study English, but back then, even the English learned Latin and Greek. Daytime was for work, and at night, he stayed up late reading books.

Through self-study, Livingston read many large books on Latin. He read extensively on science.

Later, he desired to serve humanity by sharing knowledge, so he began studying medicine. He also began learning Greek.

When he was a student at the University of Glasgow, he worked as a laborer in a factory during the holidays to save money.

Driven by his desire, he endured various hardships and earned his degree from the university.

He spent his life working for the welfare of the underprivileged. When he was in Egypt, he was often seen tending cattle or plowing fields. He took pride in working hard and didn't rely on others for service.

In the 18th century, a great man named John Howard helped reduce the brutal treatment of prisoners in Britain. The government and the country's scholars adopted his ideas and reforms. No hardship or obstacle could stop him from his mission. His strength and belief brought him victory—not just talent or language skills.

*****

VIII
Money

The right to become wealthy and prosperous belongs to the greatest of scholars and saints. They understand how to use money properly.

The progress of the pious, the hardworking, and the diligent is inevitable, while that of others is not.

Do not wish to remain poor if you are pious and knowledgeable. You must become wealthy, because you know how to spend money wisely.

If a greedy, narrow-minded person accumulates money, their earnings hold no value.

Earning money for a noble cause is akin to worship. In truth, this is the highest form of worship.

What will you use to serve humanity? Money, of course.

Earning money in the name of God will make you one of the greatest saints. You also need money to support your wife and children. It is your duty to improve the well-being of your family; failing to do so is a wrongdoing.

Show respect for money. Thoughtful and knowledgeable individuals do not look down on money.

If you spend money carelessly and without consideration, it will destroy your wisdom and principles. Do not hate money, and do not degrade yourself by harboring an unjust attachment to it.

A wise and frugal person cannot be careless with their spending. They think about the future and suppress desires for temporary comforts and pleasures, planning instead for the colder days ahead.

Those who are reckless with their spending and indulge their senses like fools disgrace their humanity.

Suffering after pleasure, unrest, and pain drain much of their energy.

If a person spends thoughtfully, their sorrow is greatly reduced. People create their own suffering by impoverishing themselves.

Those in poverty do not have the freedom of mind. If you are frugal, your mental freedom will grow.

This is not an easy task. It does not require less effort. Many people become alarmed when they see the flaws in their character, but they do not find it shameful to be frugal. In fact, being truthful is one of life's greatest virtues, and being frugal is equally important.

Those whose poverty cannot be alleviated remain small forever. During times of famine, they are the first to perish. You hold a high position in society today—what will happen to your wife and children if you suddenly die? Strive to improve your current financial situation; do not waste all your money and reduce yourself to the mercy of others.

I am not saying that you should abandon life's sweet and beautiful qualities to accumulate money like a demon. What I say is, be cautious to protect yourself from danger, and keep your mental freedom intact. If poverty keeps you occupied, your mental strength will fade. Sacrifice your own desires.

The greatest works in the world have been carried out by thrifty people or with their assistance. A person in poverty can only be concerned with their own lack—they cannot contribute to society. They feel no discomfort in spending money for good causes.

One evening, I saw an unfamiliar woman suddenly enter our house. When I asked her reason, she said she had borrowed money from someone but could not pay it back. She had met that person on the street and, fearing him, took shelter here.

How much sorrow would it cause if you were in a similar situation? If you have borrowed money from someone or have anything owed to you, no matter how small, you will feel a sense of shame before that person. This is a very painful and bothersome situation in life. If you have humanity within you, do not drag yourself into such a shameful situation.

If you have no money, it is of no use to feel sorry for yourself inwardly. I once saw a gentleman who gave away everything he had to a person in distress, and found himself in a difficult situation as a result.

If you have no money, you will have to stand helpless in front of those in need.

If you want to make your life independent, start saving, even if only a little. Do you know that Hazrat Muhammad (PBUH) used to extract oil from a lamp wick?

Hazrat Isa (Jesus) said, "Do not discard the small things, collect them."

Do not despise a single coin! Do not think that losing a little rice or a chili is of no consequence.

Even a small handful of rice can accomplish great things.

If you desire sweets, consider whether you have money to buy rice first.

One gentleman wrote a letter to his son: "Being frugal is one of life's main virtues." Many people do not see the value in budgeting money. Do not be one of them.

Many talented people lacked this quality in their character, which is why you should not imitate their flawed habits. Had they not had these flaws, they could have contributed even more to the world.

There is no glory in following their bad habits while ignoring their good qualities. Just because the moon has spots, will you stain your body with blemishes?

Accept your current circumstances and live through them. Do not exceed your limits just because things are difficult. As long as your income does not increase, you must live like the poor. You cannot deny your present reality. If your income is small, you must accept it and not spend beyond your means. Accept your present reality as the truth.

If you reject your present circumstances, you will either become a thief or rely on others. Until you are capable of giving, stand within your limits.

It is not enough to be content with your current state; you must save a little. Even a small amount of saving is necessary. Just as survival is necessary, saving is equally important. Forget the existence of what you save, and do not share it with others.

When you are impoverished—when your hardships are endless—what is the use of blaming yourself for your foolishness? Perhaps, at one point, your wife and children were happy with your generosity, but in your time of hardship, they will say, "Why did you listen to our requests, when you knew better?" They will not remain silent in your time of need; they may even complain, because they are no longer living a life of comfort.

Poverty turns people into beasts. They behave cruelly to their spouses, children, relatives, and friends, without realizing it.

Your stinginess may upset one person, but if they are hungry and you do not feed them, they might even harm you.

If you stop wasting money on trivial things, you might be able to use it to lay the foundation for something significant.

You cannot die just because others don't recognize you. Very few people in the world understand the suffering of others. Therefore, be cautious.

A father's hard-earned wealth is enjoyed by many children, while others squander it due to their own faults.

If the money earned through the labor of others is gained without effort, then national life becomes weak. People stop working hard and fail to be frugal.

It is true that a heartless rich oppressor cannot bear the suffering of a hungry, oppressed, and poor person.

Do not tell anyone about your miserable condition. It will not benefit you; no one will feel pity for you. Work. If blessings and grace come, they will come from God. Trust in this.

If you are cautious about your spending, no matter how much you earn, your family will get by. You will also have the fortune to help your poor neighbors as much as you can.

I know a person who received a letter from home saying that his three brothers had no winter clothes. The man did not pay attention to this and instead bought a 10-taka shirt for himself.

In reality, such worthless people do not come to bring happiness to the world. They only create misery for others. Anyone who comes in contact with them will not escape suffering.

If people were frugal, the world's suffering would be significantly reduced. There would not be so many poor people, and we would not hear so much wailing from the people.

Before you judge whether someone is wise and truthful, try to find out whether they are frugal or not.

When giving away your daughter in marriage, along with inquiring about the groom's appearance, qualities, and education, also find out if he is careful with money. This is an important quality. Does he have a bad habit of accumulating debt?

If a groom is frugal, even if he lacks education, beauty, and talent, your daughter's family will never suffer.

Some people say that the condition of the gentleman never improves. Do not believe this. A gentleman feels disgusted at earning money unjustly or through dishonest means. That is true, but it is also wrong for him to remain in poverty out of respect for such principles. No matter what, he will bring prosperity to his miserable state. He will not beg from others. He will not sit idle, lazy, or miserly. He will earn money through honest means and spend it wisely.

Being frugal does not mean that you should become excessively stingy, causing hardship to your family. Your wisdom and judgment should regulate your spending.

Never incur debt. If you follow this one principle, you will be able to control your spending.

Just as an empty sack cannot stand upright, similarly, your straight path will not be possible if you are in debt.

If you continue to take debt, you will find yourself becoming a great liar. Your humanity will vanish, and you will become like an animal.

A gentleman once advised a young man: Do not try to settle any debt for the sake of showing off. Do not buy a shirt on credit just to keep up with others. Boldly say, "I don't need it; what I have is enough."

If you borrow money from someone who is beneath you, you will feel ashamed before them. This feeling of shame is intolerable to an independent, dignified person.

Never borrow money. Dr. Johnson said, "To borrow is to make life miserable." A poor person is already embarrassed by their own poverty. How can they help others? Along with acquiring other good qualities, make a firm resolve to avoid the habit of borrowing.

Keeping track of household income and expenses is a good practice. Do not be ashamed to write down even a single penny. By maintaining awareness of your financial situation, you will be able to spend wisely.

The Duke of Wellington kept track of his expenses personally. He said, "The head of the household must do this work himself. All debts must be paid by him personally."

The American statesman Washington was not ashamed to keep track of his income and expenses.

When an impulse arises in your mind, suppress it. Many people and families have been destroyed because they could not control their impulses. Character strength is required to control the mind. This strength must be acquired through self-discipline. If you keep indulging in your desires, you will weaken gradually. The desires of the senses have no end, just as the cessation of worldly pleasures has no limit.

To be virtuous is a discipline—being frugal is also a discipline. People who are wasteful and in debt are never considered dignified by wise individuals. Wearing leftover clothes from a shop may preserve your outward civility, but in the eyes of wisdom and conscience, it is not civility at all. Your conscience will tell you that this is nothing but disgrace.

*****

IX

The Dignity of Life

What brings dignity? Expensive clothes? A car or a horse? A grandfather's title? No, it's not that.

Dignity is not found in such things. What I want to know is whether you are of good character! Whether you are a worshiper of truth! Whether you are a servant of knowledge!

You have a lot of money. You do not look at people with respect. When people's humanity comes into your touch, it gets ruined — I do not respect you.

Sadi says — A gentleman is one who worships truth. He respects humanity — his character and nobility are his glory.

I do not wish to hear whether you eat meat or kheer (sweet rice) every day. I do not need to know whether you have acquaintances with many people. Even if I hear that your father was a judge, my heart will not be happy. I want to see you, your inside and outside, your humanity and character. Not yours.

You have a hundred servants at home, and your tenants are scared to see you — hearing this will not make my heart happy! I do not care whether all your relatives are wealthy. What benefit will I gain from hearing this? I want to see you, your inside and outside, your humanity, your true worth.

Have you stolen money in broad daylight? If so, may your mother bless you, and may God do good for you. Your father lovingly embraces you. People admire you. Respectable people desire you. My heart will not bow to you; in contempt, I will say, "Go away."

Your soul is pure, you are a servant of knowledge, you find joy in the study of creation's diversity, your character is elevated. Following great people is your life's goal, you are victorious in self-discipline, you stand against lies and sin, you see religion as your vision deepens day by day, your soul is alert like a deer, eager, attentive — I bow to you with reverence.

You are a liar, your heart is narrow, it is uncertain whether you even have a soul, you are like a lifeless being, riding on time, you are foolish, you bring pain to others, you feel no shame in taking others' money, you are your father's firstborn — I hate you. What value do your worship and fasting hold?

You have struggled to make your life sweet and pure — sitting on torn cloth, you are engaged in the search for mysteries, the people of the world do not respect you, but I do.

You are virtuous and truthful, a seeker of knowledge, and you despise sin, whatever work you do, you believe your dignity is great.

To preserve the purity of the soul, keeping the mind free from falsehood is religion — you are truly religious, therefore the respect is yours.

You do not have a watch on your hand, you do not wear expensive clothes, you do not have foreign shoes — what harm is there? Do you have greatness within you? Those men, dressed in strange clothes, will be humbled in front of you by modesty and devotion.

If you cannot become a high-ranking government official, it does not mean your life has no value. Do not harbor such low thoughts in your heart. Remember, the king, the maharaja, or the high-ranking government officials are your servants. The one who rides in a car or on horseback, who lives in a palace, whose head constantly exudes the fragrance of flowers, whose ten servants come running at his signal, who climbs on people's backs and has people open his shoes for him, who sits on the shoulders of others to enjoy the breeze—do not be intimidated by seeing him.

*****

X

Employment, Work and Business; Initiative, Effort, and Hard Work

Employment is a noble pursuit when it serves the nation and does not diminish one's dignity or personality. When employment becomes merely a means of livelihood, when it is not seen as service to the country, do not engage in it. If you must regard your superior as more important than truth and the law, then step aside. If you cannot speak the truth fearlessly in front of your master, and if you lack the courage to resign from your job when needed, then it is clear that you are only working to pass time.

If you cannot preserve the freedom of your mind, there will be no distinction between you and an animal. Your life will be a lie. A free heart is a servant of truth. Being a blacksmith is also good—just don't make yourself a machine.

A wise and virtuous person is deeply ashamed of losing their personality—they consider it a sin.

Do you desire to become rich by earning money through unethical means in your job? A grocer is better than you. The money of the temple is pure.

There are many young people who believe that simply obtaining a job is enough to secure a position in society! Whether by theft or by unethical methods, they see no harm in it.

Your character is spotless. Earning money through small tasks will not tarnish your reputation. Those who live through theft and wrongdoing are the ones who ruin their dignity. Do not earn money through unethical means, and do not resort to lies. Never cause harm to others in order to amass wealth.

The great philosopher Plato, while traveling in Egypt, used to sell oil on his head to earn money for his travel expenses. It is the dishonest, the corrupt, and the thieves who are lowly. Business or small independent work does not diminish a person's worth; dishonesty, cunning, and deceit are what make one low. Are you spending month after month as a lackey, afraid that your honor will be tarnished? Where is your honor? Have you truly found it?

The money you earn through honest means will not lead to the fall of your soul. Your soul will only fall through laziness and dishonesty. Your work will be glorious through your touch.

Just as people from my country go to Britain these days, people from Britain once traveled to Greece.

Has anyone seen a man who returned from Britain making money by pulling bricks or working as a porter? Scholars from Britain acquired immense knowledge by traveling through different countries. Upon returning from Greece, they began to do tasks that you and I would be ashamed to do. But did their reputation suffer? A person with knowledge and virtue may remain humble for a while, but people will respect him and lift him up.

You must believe that work does not lower one's status. Work becomes dishonorable only when deceit enters into it; at no other time.

The blessings of civilization that you are enjoying—how did they come about? Was it not through your own hands? Work should not be seen as a game. Show respect for the blacksmith's sweat, the minister's hammer, the porter's shovel.

Many people say that there is no work for them. Whatever they do, wherever they walk, they only face failure. It is those who are ignorant who say such things. Their failure is their own fault. This despair and complaint comes from their lack of attention and laziness.

Dr. Johnson, with only a few pennies, came to London and never begged from anyone. Once, a friend gave him a pair of shoes, but he threw them away on the road in insult. With effort, hard work, and initiative, all obstacles are overcome. Those with virtue and diligence do not suffer. Johnson often went to bed hungry at night, but he was never upset, disheartened, or hopeless. He overcame all obstacles like a brave hero, and the principles he left behind are ones that many scholars could never achieve.

Even with virtue, success cannot be achieved without effort. Mr. Irving said, "Sitting quietly won't help you."

Try—move—just like some women can make something happen within. What is the use of barking like a dog or lying down like a lion?

You failed the exam, and now you feel like you're worth nothing. I ask, why? Don't you know that the most inexperienced people in this world are earning thousands of dollars a month?

Your pain and sorrow come from your ignorance. Do you not believe that a man can extract gold from sand? You are like a fool—lacking initiative, a wretched person devoid of self-confidence.

Whether the work is small or large, do it with all your heart and soul. Do not disdain work because of worthless friends. Strive to make your work beautiful in all ways.

Once, a gentleman told Mr. Fox, "Your writing is not good." Mr. Fox, paying full attention to the art of writing, began studying like a schoolboy, and within a short time, his writing became excellent.

The key to improvement is focus and attention. A gentleman owned a piece of land. The land was not yielding any profit, and was even incurring losses day by day. In desperation, he leased the land to someone for a nominal fee. After a few years, the lessee said, "If you wish to sell the land, give it to me. I have been able to accumulate a lot of money from it." The landowner, surprised, asked, "How could you make money from this land, which I couldn't even make a penny off of?" The lessee replied, "I am not as inattentive as you. I know no other way than hard work. I do not have the habit of sleeping until 10 a.m."

A young man once asked Mr. Scott for some advice. Mr. Scott gave him this advice: "Don't be lazy. Whatever you have to do, start now. If you need rest, do it after completing your work."

Those who use their time well will always succeed. Time is money, and even more valuable than money. Improve your life, work hard, acquire knowledge. Fix your character. Do not waste time like a miser; take your dues from time. If you waste an hour a day, think of how much time you have wasted in a year.

Look at how much work you've done in an hour each day. You will be surprised. Every day, write a little—no more than ten lines—and at the end of the year, you will have written a neat and beautiful book. If you use your life well, you will find that death will carry your achievements far and wide. If you spend your life in laziness, doing nothing, at the end of your life, it will seem like you have done nothing but play a false role—a collection of endless sorrow and complaints. If, at the end of life, you ask yourself, "What have I done in my life? Nothing!" what good will that be?

At the beginning of any task, think about whether you are fit for the work, whether you are prepared to do something that will satisfy your soul.

Progress can only be achieved through truth and virtue, and not through anything else. When you focus on truth and virtue in business, your success is inevitable. You may earn short-term gains through cheating, but those gains will be fleeting. Those who have progressed in business have never resorted to lies or cheating. Business, when done well, is honorable, but dishonor comes through dependency, lies, and unethical practices.

A man once could not bear the shame of his petty life and committed suicide. Before his death, he wrote a note saying, "This life is unbearable for me." We feel no pity for his death. He was so lowly and small that he had no right to live as a petty merchant. There is no dishonor in work or business. The famous Nawab family of Dhaka, which is well-known in Eastern Bengal, was founded by Alimullah, who was a businessman. The welfare of the nation has often come through business. Anyone who does not respect business is ignorant. One of the reasons for the greatness of the English nation is business. Without it, they would not have reached such heights.

If you buy something and think it is correct, never sell it to others. Never cheat an experienced buyer. You may feel you lost out, but wait—let your virtue and reputation spread. The disadvantages of loss will soon fill your pocket.

Maintaining virtue in business requires a great deal of humanity. A businessman who controls his greed and protects his reputation shows great character. Sweetness, patience, courtesy, and a desire for modest profits will make your business life successful.

Employment, the unending desire for jobs—young people are making their lives miserable by chasing after a life of gold through endless job seeking. Are the blacksmith, the carpenter, and the tailor truly low-class people? Are they uneducated and, therefore, not worthy of a place in civilized society? Have you ever thought about how much knowledge, thought, and effort those people put into their work? An educated person, no matter what work they do, will earn both respect and money. Do not waste the boundless power of your soul by being a beggar.

*****

XI
Character and Moral Strength

Rai Narendra Nath Sen would say, "Asia is superior to Europe in spirituality. Europe should learn spirituality from Asia." I still do not understand the meaning of this statement. If spirituality is something distinct from knowledge, character, humanity, and deeds, then it is of no use.

Where does the value of a person lie? In their character, humanity, and deeds. In reality, when we speak of character, we are referring to the best aspects of a person's life. Without character, there is nothing for a person to be proud of. If human respect is to be earned, it is earned only through character. If a person respects others, it is solely because of their character. There is no need for anyone to bow their head before another for any other reason.

The glory of all the great men born in this world lies in this very moral strength of character. When someone is said to have character, it does not mean they are perfect. It means they are truthful, humble, and respectful of knowledge. They are compassionate towards others, just, and embarrassed by the denial of rightful freedom and personality.

Having character does not mean you avoid talking to foolish people. If you are afraid to speak boldly to others, you have no character. A person of character is always courageous and fearless. They fear their own innate wisdom or conscience more than they fear others. They always keep an eye on their own deeds and words. Even if others do not know their faults, they themselves feel shame for them. A person of character feels embarrassed to show respect to a tyrant or a criminal. A truthful person is the one worthy of respect. They are always self-aware.

You will have character. All your goals in life will be focused on cultivating character. You will focus on controlling your mind, rebelling against falsehood and sin, and striving for human greatness in this pursuit. What else is there in life that could possibly be an essential need?

Money and wealth are not the goal of life. If wealth is based on lies and injustice, you should throw it away in disgust into the forest and wilderness, letting your eyes be filled with rage.

The person with character is the one worthy of respect. They are the true gentleman — the knowledgeable, humble, and truthful person.

In your home, do not insult others while flaunting your pride. You cannot call yourself a gentleman just because your father was a judge during the Nawabi era.

Are you truthful? Do you feel disgusted by speaking ill of others? Do you feel ashamed of tarnishing your own soul? Are you an enemy of injustice? Do you constantly strive to gain new knowledge? Is your behavior always sweet with others? Do you have no hesitation in showing yourself as you are? I salute you; I do not ask your father's name, I respect your greatness.

One day, a young man gave a coin to a truck driver and asked for a ticket and two annas in change. The driver returned fourteen paise instead of two annas and told him, "You may get off."

The young man said, "I do not wish to stain my hand; here is your remaining money. You steal everything, and I cannot take even single Paisa."

A person of character, indeed, hates lies and deceit. Just because you have tricked others, don't think of yourself as clever. If you have traveled by train without a ticket, consider yourself a lowly person. The guard may not have noticed you, but your conscience has witnessed your lowliness in silence.

By deceiving others to earn money, you have declared yourself a thief. By neglecting your duties and collecting people's money in a shameful way, I know you are low. If you gain self-satisfaction by performing religious rites with money gained through bribery, know this: your conscience laughs within, saying that the religious deeds of a thief are of no value.

In medieval Europe, there was an order of knights. They traveled from country to country to serve the destitute and oppressed. To protect the honor of suffering women, they were willing to give up their lives if needed. They knew no other way than justice and truth. Apart from knights, there is no one who embodies the idea of a character-rich person. Keeping your character spotless and leading a life full of truthfulness, decency, justice, and moral strength should be your vow. Greed will not tempt you off your righteous path. Before your invincible character, sin, lowliness, and weakness will crumble, and then you will be a true gentleman.

The person with an elevated character — the true gentleman — is one who knows where honor lies and how it is lost. He does not hesitate to reveal his greatness out of fear of losing respect. He understands well where and in what honor resides. The King of Sicily and Naples was once passing by a road when he saw a man with a load standing by. Many people passed by, but none would lift the load onto the man's head out of fear of losing their own honor. The emperor, however, personally lifted the load onto the man's head and gained inner satisfaction. Those who passed by without helping the man lost their honor.

A man, sweating, came to stand beside you. Would you not rise from your seat to offer it to him, regardless of how small he is? That would show your greatness. Has your humanity not taught you this? Religion is but another name for humanity.

You do not need to sacrifice your life for others. Just remove their small sufferings, offer them a little happiness, and say a kind word to them. A small gesture, like casting a sympathetic glance at a helpless person on the road, would be enough.

Sometimes, in the lower classes, we see greatness that mesmerizes our hearts. Once, a traveler named Park was exhausted and hungry while in Africa. He had sought shelter from many places, but none offered him any. As evening approached, Park feared he would either die from hunger or fall victim to a wild animal. At that moment, a poor, uncivilized woman approached and said, "You seem to be a weary traveler. Please come to our little hut. We will feed you with what little we have." The helpless traveler was saved by the hospitality of this uncivilized woman.

Park had nothing with him. On his coat, he had just four silver buttons. When he left, he took two of those buttons off and gave them to the woman as a reward for her kindness and humanity.

A person with character, a person endowed with humanity, feels more restless at another's lack than at their own. They take pride in hiding their own sufferings for the sake of others' grief. Once, a young man, in need, went to a gentleman asking for a job. The gentleman, in need of someone, looked at him and saw another young man present. Upon talking, the first young man learned that his new friend was in even more dire need. So, he hid his own need and told the gentleman that he no longer required the job. The second young man was hired instead.

A person with strong character holds justice in higher regard than even humanity. For the sake of justice and truth, they are willing to face any danger. They can renounce wealth, assets, and even family and friends, but they cannot disobey the voice of their conscience. Kazi Giyasuddin had ridiculed the fear of the emperor. When the son of King Henry IV raised his fist to the judge for the release of his guilty friend, the righteous judge paid no heed to the prince's words. Fearlessly, he ordered his staff, "Take the disrespectful prince to jail."

How does one develop a noble and righteous character? It requires practice. Perhaps you are accustomed to telling lies, and you cannot even recognize when you are speaking falsely. If you suddenly make a vow to never speak a lie again from tomorrow, you will find it hard to keep that promise.

Habits are powerful—taking them away suddenly is difficult. In the pursuit of becoming human, you must also be patient and resilient. Do you wish to become truthful? Then decide that, at least once a week, you will not tell a lie. Train yourself to speak only the truth for six months, and then, on an auspicious day, vow that you will speak no lies for two days a week. A year from now, you will find that speaking the truth comes much easier to you. Through consistent effort, there will come a day when you will not be able to lie, even if you wanted to. Never think that you will suddenly conquer your vices and desires in your struggle to improve yourself—such an approach will lead to failure.

You may be very talkative—accustomed to speaking endlessly. Slowly, practice speaking less. If you want to gain any virtue, don't rush it. You cannot become a great person suddenly—that is impossible. Bringing the mind under control is a difficult task. Gradually, pull yourself towards improvement. Do not despair during your efforts, but keep trying, and you will triumph. In your practice, you will stumble many times, but do not be afraid.

If your greed is very strong, and you always wish to take more than your share, try this—make a habit of giving some of your favorite things to a child, animal, bird, or dog without eating them yourself. Do this occasionally, and you will not only weaken your greed but also develop the habit of enduring personal hardship for the happiness of others. Without practice, the mind cannot be improved, nor can one develop noble qualities. When your heart does not become weary in giving happiness to others, you will truly be a great person. Always remember that small practices and victories lay the foundation for larger triumphs.

When someone slaps one cheek, you are not instructed to turn the other cheek. However, you should never hesitate to make sacrifices within your capacity, as much as is possible for a person of dignity. Do not try to become a gentleman just by wearing clean clothes and sitting people down in a humble room. There are other ways to become a true gentleman.

You must gradually elevate your soul. With concentration and insight, free yourself from all faults. The blessing and favor of a teacher are of no value. You are your own greatest teacher. A guru cannot give freedom; you are the owner of your own liberation. If you do not accept this, it means that your soul is dead. When a nation becomes blind, it starts invoking the name of the guru more frequently, completely denying their own soul.

Develop your character—lie, deceit, injustice, disrespect for others' feelings, indifference, rudeness, and selfishness will all vanish. A religious and spiritual person is not a mysterious being.

A person who is deceitful, selfish, deceitful with words, a thief, one who robs others' happiness and wealth, or a bribe-taker will not gain anything from their worship or fasting. God will not forget them. God does not seek the worship of such people. He desires humanity. Only by practicing humanity and being compassionate, wise, perceptive, thoughtful, and rational, one can reach liberation. Such a person will never follow religion blindly. A father may stop a child from running in the sun, and the child, out of respect for the father's command, will refrain from running and may even shrink back from the risk of burning their house. This understanding is essential for the soul's progress.

When a person becomes of noble character, an invincible power of virtue emerges within them. This power cannot be suppressed. When every person of a nation becomes of noble character, the power of the nation becomes extraordinary. The source of unshakable strength is character. Never think that there is any connection between intelligence and character. If someone is a fool but has good character, there is no contradiction. If you find a person of good character among the illiterate, understand that they may not have acquired bookish knowledge, but they have attained the true purpose of knowledge. Without reading, they are still great.

The Muslim nation became great because of its character; now, as it has lost its character, it has fallen into decline. When we see qualities like wisdom, humanity, and insight within a nation, we call it civilized and great. The true meaning of the civilization of a fallen nation is to uplift people to a higher life, to make them think in a progressive way, and to turn them into generous, righteous servants of justice.

*****

XII

Physical Labor

The headmaster of a school could make excellent houses. I knew a man who could make chairs and benches.

If you learn to make the things needed for your household with your own hands, the quality of your life will improve.

There is no shame in manual work; this should be said again and again. What is the use? Shame comes with lies and with baseness.

Once a man proudly told me, "I never go to the market." I must tell you that he was an incapable person.

Knowing how to build fences, repair houses, sweep the floor, or make tools—these are the qualities of life. If you take pride in not knowing how to do these things, I will call you a fool. What earns respect? Knowledge, character, and humanity. There is no respect in not knowing how to handle the practical matters of life.

If you don't know how to cook, will you be called brave? Will people say, "There is no one as gentlemanly as you"?

If your condition is poor, if you are pious, noble, wise, and feel shy about doing household chores, I do not consider you inferior.

Once, a schoolboy used to give the money he earned from cutting rice in December to poor students. Isn't this a very noble example?

In the village, a poor man's house leaks during the monsoon—oh, how much suffering! If you ten people were to repair his house, your respect would not decrease. But you lack the skills and heart to do so.

Is it always possible to help someone with money? Though verbal sympathy is not worth a penny.

Strive to be great; don't degrade your humanity by imitating incapable people. Don't let your head bow only in front of money and buildings.

There is a story: the enemy was coming to capture the Nawab, but the Nawab couldn't escape because there was no one to help him wear his shoes. How do you regard this Nawab?

Once, I heard about fifty or sixty schoolboys who were digging a water canal with hoes and spades. Whenever I think of this, immense joy fills my heart. I once saw a noble person selling needles, thread, and tea to laborers in Kolkata. He had no trace of arrogance in his nature—I respect him.

When you are a schoolboy, you can learn many practical household tasks alongside your studies. There is no harm in keeping a small toolbox with a hammer, a chisel, and a saw beside your books. When the great scientist Newton was a boy, he had a hammer and saw beside his books. If you don't feel like studying, take up the hammer and work. Every Sunday, you can go home and learn carpentry; it won't diminish your respect.

Fear the criticism of incapable people. Who are they? Those who will remain small forever.

There is a blacksmith's house near yours. What harm is there in learning how they make hoes, how they heat red-hot iron, and how they hammer it to make sparks fly?

Knowing how to cook, how to draw water from the well with a pitcher—there is no dishonor in these skills. Don't be ashamed of getting dressed while your wife is sick and the servant is absent.

There is no honor in having servants cook for you or do the work.

It is better to handle the work yourself if you can, rather than keeping servants. The belief that the more servants a person has, the more they are considered a gentleman, only exists in the minds of uncivilized people.

There is no dishonor in learning all the various tasks necessary to run a household. Always remember that your respect is based on truth and humanity. Never fear a person who is without thought or character in their actions. Wait, and people will eventually imitate you.

*****

XIII

The Value of Word - Keeping Promises

There is value in a person's words. Only a true gentleman can fully understand this. How much of a gentleman you are can be understood from the value of your words.

You may not be able to go into the forest like Lord Shri Ram to uphold the truth of your father, but in your everyday life, can you not uphold the value of your small, everyday words? If you have promised a gentleman that you will meet him at 2:00 p.m. tomorrow, then you must meet him at that exact time because you are a gentleman, and your words have worth.

If you have said that you will pay a creditor on a certain day, and that person has been coming to your door every day, dry-mouthed, hoping for your kindness, and you keep making new promises, you are a fraud and a coward. If you are penniless, declare your situation openly, and ask for forgiveness from your creditor, no matter how small he may be. He will not be able to do anything to harm you, and that is the truth. At the very least, people will know you are not a liar.

A civilized nation is not made only by tall buildings and wealth. Along with buildings and wealth, there is another great aspect of civilization, and that is the value of one's words.

If you cannot uphold the value of your words, do not speak them. Never disgrace your tongue. There is no greater cowardice than this.

Words that are associated with injustice should rarely be spoken—it's better to talk too much than to speak unjustly. A chatterer is a worthless person, and he harms himself. He does not deceive society like a liar or someone who disrespects their tongue.

An English gentleman had captured a thief. The thief begged for mercy, saying, "If you promise not to betray us, if you don't inform the authorities about us, I will take you to your home." It was the thief's rule to kill every prisoner. The English gentleman promised that he would never harm the thief. The thief then took the Englishman to his house at night. The Englishman secretly sent word to the police and had the thief arrested. He said, "A thief's promise has no value."

The gentleman had certainly shown cowardice. You must uphold the value of your words. Wise individuals from all countries speak little, make few promises, and work much.

*****

XIV

Fiery Temper

Responding impatiently to words, becoming enraged over trivial matters, is a characteristic of barbaric nations. What use are past civilizations, written knowledge, and the pretense of intellectual glory if we cannot express sweetness, humility, and politeness in all aspects of our daily lives?

Again, I say—destroying the calmness of your nature easily, responding to cruel words with even more cruel words, is not politeness; it is calmness that you should strive for. If a hand has been raised to kill, bring it down once, and think again.

Those who become enraged upon hearing opposing views, use foul language, and, if they have the power, are not ashamed to kill their opponent—these are the signs of a deeply uncivilized and barbaric individual.

A nation that enforces intolerant rule over its people will inevitably find itself in a lower place.

Whether in a village or a high society, never allow your nature to run wild—be cautious!

Do you not feel ashamed to speak cruel words and raise your eyes in anger? This is the work of low-class individuals!

A nation that does not know how to speak in a civilized and polite manner is extremely degraded. They will forever lose the respect for humanity in the hearts of others.

In every task, you can see a person's work ethic and devotion! You must believe this.

In youth, a great temptation arises to establish your own importance in the eyes of others—to spread your own glory and dignity far and wide. The soul's base desires must be forcefully crushed.

Those who have not learned to be tolerant and patient have no right to be considered virtuous.

You are a shopkeeper, and a customer comes to buy goods from you—no matter how much the customer may annoy you, never become intolerant and use rude language toward them. If you do, then I will consider you a coward. Do not become enraged at a single opposing word, do not let a small insult heat your temper—wait, be patient, your humility will win.

*****

XV
Ideal - Living Ideal

I do what I see. — What I hear, I do not feel like doing. For how long have I been reading in books that one should not lie, yet this bad habit still hasn't left me? I don't even realize that this is a bad habit.

Once, a boy blamed his mother, saying, "You are lying, you are telling lies." The mother, with disdain, retorted, "How could I, being so small, tell a lie?" Upon seeing his mother's contemptuous expression, the boy realized how small a lie truly is.

If you do not worship—if you stay with loving and devoted people, you too will be inclined to love God.

Read the biographies of great people— you will wish to become great. Long ago, a young man overcame immense suffering and established himself through pain and sorrow; when you learn of it, your own sorrow will feel half as heavy.

One person used to collect trash from the streets—he did not have money to buy oil. At night, he would set fire to the trash and read books. Another youth would read books by the light of a street lamp. When you hear such stories, don't you feel empowered? Doesn't your broken spirit rise in the light of their inspiration?

Helping others is a very good thing. If this idea were only in books, perhaps only a few people would help others!

In Portsmouth, a cobbler would entice a child with money and bring him to his small shop to teach him. This humble, unfortunate man found satisfaction in doing good for humanity. His name was John Foundes. When you hear the story of this unknown great man's selfless and incredible service to humanity, does a sense of shame not arise within you?

In a province of France, there was once an immense shortage of water. The suffering of the people there was unbearable. For years, this continued, with no hope of any remedy.

In that province lived a young man named Geyo, who was of a frivolous, carefree nature. Laughter and song were his life. One day, the villagers noticed that Geyo had become unusually serious and depressed. This carefree young man, who had once laughed through life, had heard that there was no way to alleviate his homeland's water shortage without spending vast sums of money. Suddenly, a thought struck his innocent mind—could he not do something about it? From then on, he began to speak less and became more thoughtful, and his friends were amazed at his newfound seriousness.

After several years of study, Geyo started a business. Over the years, his wealth grew steadily. Gradually, Geyo's name spread as one of the wealthiest men around. Despite his enormous wealth, Geyo walked the streets in ragged clothes, and people began to call him miserly. There was ample reason for such a reputation, as with his growing wealth, his miserly nature grew as well. So much so that he never even married, afraid of spending money. Many began to despise him for his cruel lifestyle. Some even felt embarrassed to say his name aloud in the morning, lest they go hungry that day.

The children would spit at him as he passed. When Geyo became old, he had vast wealth—millions of dollars—but no one respected him. He was the most contemptible man in the country.

When Geyo died, people discovered that he had left a will. It said: "I have spent my entire life gathering wealth to relieve the water shortage of my birthplace. I vowed to solve this problem in my lifetime. I leave all my wealth to the government for this purpose."

The news spread far and wide. People came in droves to pay their respects to this great man's body. Those who had despised him now wept and honored his pure memory. Upon hearing this selfless service, does your heart not feel heavy? On the side of the road, a poor farmer is sitting with a load. You wish to help him by lifting his load, but you cannot—out of fear of ridicule from your useless friends. No one else does such a thing. You wish to imitate the simplicity and humility of great people, but you cannot because all around you, you see only luxury and indulgence. Your resolve weakens.

When you see a great man walking in ragged clothes with a smiling face, you no longer feel ashamed to wear ragged clothes yourself; rather, you feel proud! When a child is born, they are pure and innocent. As they grow older, some children take on divine qualities, while others become wicked and beastly like their parents. Who will say why a Hindu child is a Hindu? It is because they learn from what they see.

There is no greater religion than serving humanity. I can say this and I do. When I see you, working in a humble corner of the world to educate and enlighten human beings, my head bows in respect before you. I too wish to dedicate my life to serving humanity.

Novelists create great characters in their books with the intention that, by reading them, your mind will be uplifted. By following these ideals, you will desire to shape your life according to them. This is the value of novels. Even the most unfortunate person can become a better individual by reading novels. They are drawn toward greatness.

A call has come to go to war, but no one is going. Who will go to the battlefield and easily lay down their life? Someone from a group says, "I will go!" Immediately, several other youths say, "We will go too!"

You are chasing a herd of sheep to the riverbank. Despite all the fighting, not a single sheep will go into the water. You may not be able to cross the river, but then suddenly, one sheep jumps in, and one by one, the rest of the flock follows.

You have many thoughts in your mind, but you cannot act. Why? Because you have not seen anyone else doing the thing you want to do! You recognize this as your weakness, yet still, you cannot do it. What a wonder!

Doing business is good. Stop, in your meaningless job, your sorrow, pain, and poverty only increase. Yet, you cannot leave this trap to start a business because no one in your circle of friends has set an example of doing so.

You wish to stand in the market like Socrates and speak to the common people about greatness week after week. You want to invite the farmers of the village every Sunday and read the newspaper to them so they can improve their lives. You have no work of your own, the burden of an idle life has become unbearable for you, and you wish to discuss moral values with your small, lowly neighbors and teach their children, hoping that they will become better individuals in the future. But you cannot, because you have never seen anyone do these things. Your noble and great aspirations fade away like bubbles in the water.

Just as you imitate piety and greatness, you also touch the stain of sin and degradation. There was a group of friends. Among them, there was never any discussion of sinful words, and their lives were not great. But neither were they degraded. Sometimes, they would talk about good things.

Suddenly, a depraved person joined their group. To everyone's surprise, within a short time, all the young men had become degraded, speaking only of base desires and pleasures.

Your wife is extremely indulgent. She refuses to carry a pot in her hands. She eats whatever the maid prepares. She does not keep track of anything, out of fear of losing her honor. If she were to hear about the simple life of the Empress of Nasiruddin, her arrogance would lessen greatly.

How people imitate others, even to the point of giving their lives, is reflected in the following story: Once, there was a terrible storm at sea. Suddenly, a ship sank near the coast.

Who will go to rescue the passengers? Many people stood on the shore. One person, opening a boat, asked, "Who will come with me? If I must give my life, who will follow me?" One person said, "I will go." Immediately, many others said, "We will go too."

In the storm, while seeing the passengers of the sunken ship, Grace Darlington's father felt sorrow and pain, but he did not have the courage to act. When his daughter, Grace, said, "Father, I will go with you, we can save the unfortunate passengers," only then did the father take action. Together, they launched a boat into the rough waves.

In the battlefield, many soldiers lay down their lives after seeing so many others doing the same, standing in front of fire, mocking the sharp sword.

The value of living ideals is greater. Good deeds are never done in an abstract way. When we go to Britain, we find living ideals of great power that help us strengthen ourselves. It is there we go to feel the touch of power and awaken our own.

The Quran is there, but why has the Muslim nation not advanced? Why have Hindus and Muslims not become better people? How many things we hear and read, but where do good deeds come from?

What we need is a living human being, a life full of strength and ideals, whose touch awakens the spirit within us.

****

The End of the Book

www.ingramcontent.com/pod-product-compliance
Lightning Source LLC
Chambersburg PA
CBHW020503160726
47991CB00007B/2785